Keep this pocket-sized Frith
you are travelling around the
holiday.

Whether you are in your car or on foot, you will
enjoy an evocative journey back in time. Compare
the West Midlands of old with what you can see
today—see how the streets of the towns and cities
have changed, how shops and buildings have been
altered or replaced; look at fine details such as
lamp-posts, shop fascias and trade signs; and see the
many alterations to the landscapes of the region that
have taken place unnoticed during our lives, some of
which we may have taken for granted.

At the turn of a page you will gain fascinating
insights into the unique history of the West
Midlands.

FRANCIS FRITH'S
pocket ALBUM

WEST MIDLANDS

A POCKET ALBUM

Adapted from an original book by
CLIVE HARDY

FRITH
BOOK Co

First published in the United Kingdom in 2003 by
Frith Book Company Ltd

Reprinted 2003

ISBN 1-85937-719-X

British Library Cataloguing in Publication Data

West Midlands—A Pocket Album
Adapted from an original book by Clive Hardy

Frith Book Company Ltd
Frith's Barn, Teffont,
Salisbury, Wiltshire SP3 5QP
Tel: +44 (0) 1722 716 376
Email: info@francisfrith.co.uk
www.francisfrith.co.uk

Printed and bound in Great Britain by MPG, Bodmin

Front Cover: Wolverhampton Dudley Street c1900 / W285007

Frontispiece: Birmingham, New Street 1890 / B100001
*The hand-colouring is for illustrative purposes only, and is not intended to be
historically accurate.*

CONTENTS

FRANCIS FRITH
VICTORIAN PIONEER

Francis Frith, founder of the world-famous photographic archive, was a complex and multi-talented man. A devout Quaker and a highly successful Victorian businessman, he was philosophic by nature and pioneering in outlook. By 1855 he had already established a wholesale grocery business in Liverpool, and sold it for the astonishing sum of £200,000, which is the equivalent today of over £15,000,000. Now in his thirties, and captivated by the new science of photography, Frith set out on a series of pioneering journeys up the Nile and to the Near East.

INTRIGUE AND EXPLORATION

He was the first photographer to venture beyond the sixth cataract of the Nile. Africa was still the mysterious 'Dark Continent', and Stanley and Livingstone's historic meeting was a decade into the future. The conditions for picture taking confound belief. He laboured for hours in his wicker darkroom in the sweltering heat of the desert, while the volatile chemicals fizzed dangerously in their trays. Back in London he exhibited his photographs and was 'rapturously cheered' by members of the Royal Society. His reputation as a photographer was made overnight.

VENTURE OF A LIFE-TIME

By the 1870s the railways had threaded their way across the country, and Bank Holidays and half-day Saturdays had been made obligatory by Act of Parliament. All of a sudden the working man and his family were able to enjoy days out, take holidays, and see a little more of the world.

With typical business acumen, Francis Frith foresaw that these new tourists would enjoy having souvenirs to commemorate their days out. For the next thirty years he travelled the country by train and by pony and trap, producing fine photographs of seaside resorts and beauty spots that were keenly bought by millions of Victorians. These prints were painstakingly pasted into family albums and pored over during the dark nights of winter, rekindling precious memories of summer excursions. Frith's studio was soon supplying retail shops all over the country, and by 1890 F Frith & Co had become the greatest specialist photographic publishing company in the world, with over 2,000 sales outlets, and pioneered the picture postcard.

FRANCIS FRITH'S LEGACY

Francis Frith had died in 1898 at his villa in Cannes, his great project still growing. The archive he created continued in business for another seventy years. By 1970 it contained over a third of a million pictures showing 7,000 British towns and villages.

Frith's legacy to us today is of immense significance and value, for the magnificent archive of evocative photographs he created provides a unique record of change in the cities, towns and villages throughout Britain over a century and more. Frith and his fellow studio photographers revisited locations many times down the years to update their views, compiling for us an enthralling and colourful pageant of British life and character.

We are fortunate that Frith was dedicated to recording the minutiae of everyday life. For it is this sheer wealth of visual data, the painstaking chronicle of changes in dress, transport, street layouts, buildings, housing, engineering and landscape that captivates us so much today, offering us a powerful link with the past and with the lives of our ancestors.

Computers have now made it possible for Frith's many thousands of images to be accessed almost instantly. The archive offers every one of us an opportunity to examine the places where we and our families have lived and worked down the years. Its images, depicting our shared past, are now bringing pleasure and enlightenment to millions around the world a century and more after his death.

WEST MIDLANDS
AN INTRODUCTION

For a thousand years our county system had served England well, but in 1974 the Local Government Act 1972 came into effect, and with it came a radical realignment of many of our county boundaries with scant regard for history, tradition, community or identity. Among the changes, Southern Lancashire was butchered to create the Metropolitan Boroughs of Merseyside and Greater Manchester; Cumberland and Westmorland were abolished altogether; and Rutland, England's smallest county, was dragged kicking and screaming into a merger with Leicestershire. Yorkshire, our largest county, was dissected. The provisions of the Act saw the abolition of the three ridings, an administrative division that had served the county well since the days when it was ruled by its own Scandinavian kings at York. The ridings were replaced by three new counties, North Yorkshire, South Yorkshire and West Yorkshire. In addition former East and West Riding territory was hived off to create something called Humberside; Lancashire and the new county of Cumbria gained parts of the western areas of the West Riding; and a part of the North Riding which included the great steel town of Middlesborough was incorporated into the new county of Cleveland. Staffordshire, Worcestershire and Warwickshire would also be robbed of territory, as the Black Country, Birmingham, and Coventry were transferred into a new county to be known as the West Midlands. Warwickshire came out worse off. At a stroke the county lost not only a large area of territory, but its manufacturing and commercial heartland centred on Birmingham and Coventry.

The book is divided into four sections: the Black Country, Around Birmingham, Around Coventry, and Other Places. Where the Black Country begins and ends has been argued over for decades, but most people accept that it is the 100 square miles or so of territory lying within the quadrilateral Wolverhampton across to Walsall, from Walsall down to Halesowen, across to Stourbridge and back up to Wolverhampton. Those of you with other ideas can fight it out amongst yourselves. Among the places featured in this section are Wolverhampton, Bilston, Walsall, Dudley, Stourbridge and Kingswinford.

The pictures of Wolverhampton were taken between 1890 and 1910. First mentioned in its own right in 1078 and granted a weekly market in 1258, Wolverhampton was the largest borough in Staffordshire until the creation of the borough of Stoke-on-Trent in 1910. By the early decades of the 19th century access to coal, iron, and the ever expanding canal network gave Wolverhampton a competitive edge. Though famed as the centre for lock-making, the town was heavily engaged in producing a wide range of products including hinges, bolts, screws, edged tools, hammers, fire-irons, candlesticks, buckles and screws. For both home and overseas markets Wolverhampton manufacturers produced tea and coffee pots, tin plate and japanned goods, caddies and inkstands. There were also brass founders, chemical works, a munitions plant, and yarn spinning for woollen carpets. Later, when the railways came, additional jobs were brought to the town with the opening of Stafford Road Works, part of which was built on the site of the original Shrewsbury & Birmingham Railway's terminus of 1849. By the 1890s the town's population was approaching 90,000. One guide book from the period describes Wolverhampton as ' the capital of the Black Country, an extensive coal and iron mining district, in which vegetation is almost entirely replaced by heaps of slag and cinders'.

It is hard, then, to reconcile the fact that in the early 19th century Wolverhampton was still very much a market town, and the best dairy herd in the county belonged to a Mr Miller at Dunstall. Most of his milk production went for cheese, and calves were fattened to eight or ten weeks. Cows too old for the dairy or those accidently barren were fattened for the butcher. In June 1811 Miller sold some cows at Wolverhampton market. One was a six-year-old which had been milked for three summers and had calved once. The cow weighed in at 230lbs per quarter; Miller estimated that she had given sufficient milk for 480lbs of cheese a year, 120lbs of whey butter, and she had given birth to a 120lb calf.

Bilston's associations with coal mining, quarrying, smelting of iron ore, forging and so on are long. There were coal pits during the reign of Edward I, and the Reverend Richard Ames, curate of St Leonard's in the 17th century, wrote in the church register that coal had been got at Bilston since 1380. What we know for certain is that in 1490 William Tomkys, Thomas Jackson and Nycolas Foxall searched for coal in Moorfields. By 1827 Bilston pits were producing 316,000 tonnes of coal a year, thanks to the 30ft seam of Thick Coal; it was near the surface and easily accessible at Tipton and

Wednesbury. Bilston had a lock-making industry of sorts in the 16th century but it remained fairly static; along with Pontypool, Bilston was an early centre for japanning—the copying of Japanese goods by English factories.

On the other hand, the earliest that Brierley Hill is known to have been inhabited is 1619, though by the mid 18th century it too was noted for its coal pits, nail-making, brickworks, forges and glass-houses. Brierley's development was influenced by the Stourbridge and Dudley Canals, cut in the 1770s and 1780s to provide Stourbridge glass works with Dudley coal, and with access to other markets by way of a junction with the Staffs & Worcs Canal at Stourton. A further boost came in 1792 with the opening of a link between the Dudley and Birmingham Canals. The major industrial development at Brierley Hill was building the Earl of Dudley's

WOLVERHAMPTON, LICHFIELD STREET 1910 / W285004

Round Oak Iron Works in the 1850s. Though by no means the first iron works in the area, it would become the most important. It was constructed on the opposite side of the canal to the New Level Furnaces and adjacent to the tracks of the recently opened Oxford, Worcester & Wolverhampton Railway. Production began at Round Oak in 1857, and as demand grew the works was gradually extended. In 1889 a chain works was commissioned, and in 1892 Round Oak switched over to producing steel. Our pictures of Brierley Hill were taken in the 1960s, a time when Round Oak was one of the most modern steel plants in the West Midlands and capable of producing in excess of 250,000 tonnes a year.

Stourbridge came into existence at a crossing point of the Stour.

STOURBRIDGE, KING EDWARD VI GRAMMAR SCHOOL c1955 / S213004

By the end of the 14th century it had its own market, and during the 16th century refugees from Hungary and Lorraine established a glass industry on Lye Waste, thanks to the quality of the local fireclay. The seams between Stourbridge and Gornalwood would prove to be the most important in the Black Country. Writing in 1817 in his book 'Topographical History of Staffordshire', William Pitt describes Stourbridge fireclay. 'The clay possesses this peculiar excellency, that a pot made of it, with a proper heat, will melt almost anything into glass, provided it be fluxed with proper salts'. Some of these clay pots were huge, holding 1.5 tonnes. Their life span was determined very much by their size, anything from one to twelve months, and a ready supply of quality fireclay on the doorstep would see the glass industry entrenched in the area.

AROUND BIRMINGHAM

Birmingham was first visited by a Frith cameraman in 1890. Redevelopment of the town centre began in the 1850s and continued into the 1880s. It was a two-fold plan. First and foremost it aimed to give Birmingham a grand civic area as befitting one of the country's leading industrial and commercial towns. Among the buildings erected, the Birmingham and Midland Institute, Paradise Street, opened in 1856. Its metallurgical school became one of the most important in the 19th century, and it was also famed for its penny lectures. Among the visiting lecturers were the likes of Charles Dickens, who gave some of his earliest public lectures here to help raise funds for the Institute. Other visitors included T H Huxley and Anthony Trollope. The university, or Mason College as it was then called, was built between 1875-80 at a cost of £60,000 and was endowed by Sir Josiah Mason with a further £140,000. The

Grand Hotel, Colmore Row was completed in 1875, the first meeting in the council chamber of the new Council House took place in November 1878, and the Art Gallery and Museum opened in 1885. A school of art was also opened in 1885, and a technical school in 1896. A new County Court building was opened in 1882, and in 1889 Birmingham was elevated to city status. The granting of an Assize was, however, dependent upon the city having suitable courts. Sir Aston Webb and Ingress Bell were commissioned to design the Victoria Law Courts, Corporation Street.

Secondly, redevelopment would rid the town centre of a slum district that covered 93 acres. Joseph Chamberlain introduced improvement schemes—they were badly needed, for between 1871 and 1875 the death rate within the Birmingham slum area was 3.2

BIRMINGHAM, THE COUNCIL HOUSE 1896 / 37277

per cent above the national average. Health inspectors, recruited in the late 1870s in an effort to raise standards, found that the wells used by 60,000 people in the slum area were contaminated with either raw sewerage or other substances. As befitting Birmingham's status, a new principal thoroughfare was to be driven through the slum area. There would also be a number of new side and connecting streets, such as one from Monmouth Street along the side of St Philip's Church and across Temple Row. A new link would also be cut across John Street to the junction of Dale End and Coleshill Street, while a further link would cut across Little Cherry Street and Crooked Lane to the High Street. If all went well, the unhealthy area of Steelhouse Lane, Lancaster Street, Stafford Street, and Aston Lane from Steelhouse Lane to Costa Green would soon be but a memory. The new street (Corporation Street) itself would rid the town of the evil-smelling and common lodging district around Old Square and Lichfield Street, and provide a much-needed new road out of the centre to the north-east. Of the slum area, Councillor Ward said that 'the rubbish and dilapidation of whole quarters have reminded me of Strasbourg which I saw soon after the bombardment'.

Before Birmingham received its Charter of Incorporation in 1838 it was divided into a number of districts, each of which was controlled by administrators known as Street Commissioners. They had considerable powers: they could levy taxes and appoint bailiffs. There was no audit of their dealings, and they were unaccountable to the public at large; whether or not it is true, many were considered to be corrupt, devious and without scruples - nothing new there. The Commissioners were responsible for such things as street lighting, public works and repairs, and markets. One thing the Street Commissioners did do was to build the covered market hall in Worcester Street. Designed by Charles Edge and costing £67,261, the market opened in November 1834. When our cameraman visited it in 1896 it was normal practice for fishmongers to sell fish such as Dover sole, whiting, and halibut live. On Saturday nights some traders would sell off perishables cheaply to the poor. This could be a bit of a free-for-all; a Mr Mountford, a butcher, said that he often had to defend his wife and himself from 'thugs' when he did it.

By 1906 Birmingham was described as 'the fourth town of England in size and population (522,182 inhabitants in 1901), and the see of an Anglican (since 1905) and of a Roman Catholic bishop, standing on a series of gentle hills in the N W corner of Warwickshire. In plan it is irregular, and many of its older streets are narrow and crooked: but the modern business thoroughfares are broad and handsomely built. It is the chief centre in England, if not the world, of the manufacture of brass, iron, and other metallic wares of all kinds, and it is the most important industrial town in England after Manchester. In spite of its numerous tall chimneys and often smoky atmosphere, Birmingham has the reputation of being healthier than most large manufacturing towns'. What is surprising is that given the conditions prevailing in the slum area there was never a major outbreak of cholera. There were several deaths during an outbreak in 1832, and in July 1865 there were 243 inmates in the local workhouse with symptoms, but all recovered. Outbreaks of smallpox seem to have had higher casualty rates. There was an epidemic in 1884 in which 1591 cases were reported.

AROUND COVENTRY

The origins of Coventry are obscure, but in all probability it began in the 7th century with the establishment of a hamlet to serve an Anglo-Saxon convent; both were destroyed by the Danes in 1016. In 1043 Leofric, Earl of Mercia, and Lord of Couentrev, founded a

Benedictine Priory which he endowed with half his land in the town - hence the division of the town into the Prior's Half and the Earl's Half, the approximate border running through Broadgate. The town itself grew up at the junction of the roads to Warwick, Lichfield, Leicester and London, and its first golden age would dawn during the 14th century.

By this time Coventry's trade was founded on wool, leather goods, metal working, and the manufacture of soap, but cloth was becoming increasingly important. A royal charter of incorporation was granted in 1345, by which time the town's industry and commerce was firmly in the hands of the guilds. It was the time when the two great churches of St John's and St Michael's were constructed, and a city wall three miles long, with 32 towers and 12 gates erected. A poll-tax return for 1377 gives us an estimated population of around 7000, making Coventry the fourth town in

COVENTRY, THE THREE SPIRES c1890 / C169002

England after London, Norwich and Bristol. Coventry was seen as a boom town, attracting an influx of people from surrounding villages in search of work. Immigration was even more pronounced during the Dissolution, when the enclosure of monastic and ecclesiastical estates led to a massive depopulation throughout much of Warwickshire and Northamptonshire; many came to Coventry to find work, or to beg.

The Coventry of the 18th century was still dominated by the wool trade, though by 1765 the manufacture of silk ribbons had become a major local industry and would remain so well into the 19th century. The town was also noted for watchmaking; the Chapelfields would develop into a watchmakers' district of small workshops and skilled craftsmen. In 1768 the Coventry Canal Act was passed. The two principal objectives were to link Coventry to the Grand Trunk Canal and to open up a supply line for cheap coals from the Bedworth coalfield. As there were no locks between Coventry and Atherstone, coal traffic was soon moving; even so, the authorised capital was soon spent, engineer James Brindley had be given the sack, and wrangles with other canal companies meant that the terminus at Fazeley was not reached until 1790.

By 1801 the population stood at 16,000, increasing to 30,700 by 1841 and nearly 41,000 twenty years later. The city did have physical problems in expanding. It was virtually surrounded by common fields known as the Lammas and Michaelmas lands, and this was a direct cause in the development between 1840 and 1860 of the separate township of Hillfields.

The earliest pictures of Coventry in the Frith Collection date from about 1884, though we have a more positive date of 1892, the dawn of the town's second golden age, for the bulk of them. In 1868 the Coventry Machinists' Co won an order to build 300 bicycles on sub-contract for the Paris market. The first bicycles to be made for sale originated from the Paris workshops of coach repairer Pierre Michaux. By 1865 Michaux and his sons had opened a bicycle factory and were capable of producing 400 machines a year. At the time, Coventry Machinists probably considered the sub-contract as just another job, but it was the catalyst for a whole new industry. In 1874 Ariel set up shop in Spon Street; it was the first firm to concentrate solely upon the manufacture of bicycles, and by the mid 1890s there were 80 cycle firms in and around the town. Innovations included tricycles from Humber and Coventry Lever and quadricycles from the likes of Coventry Machinists. The tandem quadricycle roadster from Coventry Machinists could even be converted into a single tricycle by removing either the front or rear wheels. Further advances came in 1896 when the Daimler Motor Syndicate moved into an old cotton mill in the town. Their first engines were not powerful enough to drive a horseless carriage, but were ideal for strapping onto bicycles; thus they played a part in the founding of the motorcycle industry, though neither Daimler nor Daimler-Benz themselves went into motorcycle production. In 1900 local firm Perks & Birch came up with a novel idea for converting the pedal cycle into a motorcycle, by fitting their motor wheel in place of the rear wheel. The Singer Co also adopted the Perks & Birch motor wheel for use in their tricycles.

At the beginning of the 20th century Coventry was being described as 'an ancient city with 69,877 inhab, in 1901, which has grown rapidly since 1875 in consequence of the enormous expansion of the cycle-manufacturing industry, of which it is the headquarters. It possesses also manufactures of motor-cars, sewing machines, ribbons and watches.' In 1904 the town received a further boost when it was selected by Courtaulds for their main plant. In 1907 there were 332 employees, by 1939 there were 5,000, and by 1963 the figure had risen to 7,000.

WOLVERHAMPTON

DUDLEY STREET c1900 / W285007

Here we see the hustle and bustle of Dudley Street at the beginning of the 20th century. High street chain stores are already in evidence: Freeman, Hardy & Willis, and H Samuel. Hyam & Co, who supplied everything for the gentleman, offered a range of footwear with unusual names: the Eric at 10s 6d a pair, the Edis at 12s 6d, and the Esmond at 14s 6d.

In the days of horse-drawn trams Darlington Street was considered wide enough for a single line only, and here inbound and outbound cars have made use of the passing loop. As can be seen, double-deck cars required a pair of horses to pull them, sometimes three if the going was particularly steep. These cars could carry about 20 passengers in the saloon and 24 on the top deck.

WOLVERHAMPTON
DARLINGTON STREET 1890 / W285003

As well as retail outlets and the main post office, there were a number of buildings along Queen Street which dated from the earlier decades of the 19th century, including the Mechanics' Institute and Athenaeum (1835); the Dispensary with its Doric demi-columns (1826); and the County Court, the ground floor of which was built in 1813, the upper storey being added in 1829.

WOLVERHAMPTON

QUEEN STREET c1900 / W285001

WOLVERHAMPTON

QUEEN SQUARE 1890 / W285006

With a DA registration plate, the automobile is from the Wolverhampton area, and appears to be chauffeur-driven. In the years immediately prior to the Great War, a number of British car manufacturers got round the problem of the poor state of most of the country's roads by offering 'colonial' versions of their touring cars. These models had greater ground clearance than vehicles manufactured for the domestic market. In 1913 Standard offered a four-wheel drive.

WOLVERHAMPTON

QUEEN SQUARE 1910 / W285002

WOLVERHAMPTON

THE MARKET 1910 / W285008

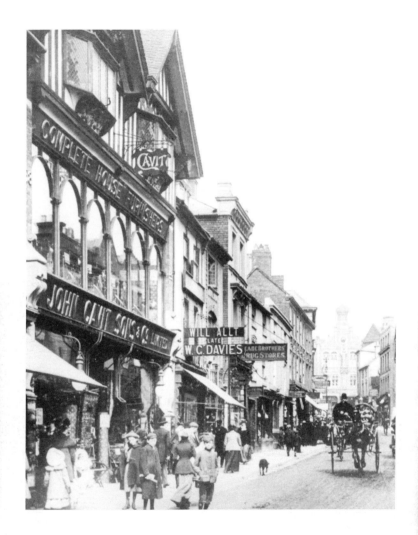

WOLVERHAMPTON

VICTORIA STREET 1910 / W285005

Just two miles from Wolverhampton, Tettenhall retained its two greens despite the Enclosure Commissioners. In AD910 Tettenhall was the scene of one of the most important battles in English history. It was here that Edward the Elder of Wessex defeated the Danes. The battle marked a turning point. From then onwards the English went over to the offensive, Edward's ultimate aim being the total reconquest of the Danelaw.

TETTENHALL

THE GREEN c1960 / T140006

As at Tipton and Wednesbury, the 30 ft seam of Thick Coal was near the surface at Bilston. Though there is evidence for coal pits at the time of Edward I, Bilston came into its own during the 19th century. In 1827 local mines produced an estimated 317,000 tonnes, and by the mid 1860s output was around 10 million tonnes. The population expanded from 6,900 in 1801 to 24,000 in 1861.

BILSTON

STREET SCENE c1960 / B353004

BILSTON

THE GREYHOUND INN c1960 / B353005

Located in the High Street, it is thought that the Greyhound Inn could be as early as the mid 15th century. Note that the gables are not in line.

A hundred years or so before this picture was taken Park Street was already a street of shops. In the 1850s Harry Grove the chemist was the place to go for Grove's tonic tincture which 'will relieve most acute pain instantaneously, arising either from a carious tooth or soreness of the gums'. Other businesses in Harry's day were Barrett's the tailors and general clothiers; the unfortunately named W Rotten (Junior), fish salesman and dealer in game and poultry; George French the auctioneer; and William Gough, saddler.

WALSALL

PARK STREET 1967 / W161018

The Bridge was a busy tram interchange and terminus. After Wolverhampton, Walsall is the largest of the Black Country towns. Between 1801 and 1901 its population rose from 10,000 to 87,000—and it is considerably higher today at over 184,000. Though famous for its leather goods, Walsall grew up on coal and ironstone mining, iron working, and limestone quarrying.

WALSALL

THE BRIDGE 1908 / W161001

WEDNESBURY

HIGH STREET c1960 / W235012

Wednesbury grew rapidly between 1851 and
1861 with the opening of firms like the Old
Park Works and Lloyds, Foster & Co.
However, during the slump of 1875-1886
the town suffered, with nine out of its eleven
iron firms going out of business. There is little
of pre-18th-century Wednesbury left save for
the parish church.

WEDNESBURY

ST PAUL'S CHURCH C1965 / W235003

West Bromwich was one of four Staffordshire county boroughs created in 1889; the others were Hanley, Walsall and Wolverhampton. Between 1801 and 1901 West Bromwich's population rose from 5,600 to over 65,000 owing to its becoming a centre for iron-making.

WEST BROMWICH

HIGH STREET 1963 / W237016

By the late 13th century both coal and ironstone were being mined in the Sedgley area, and by the end of the 17th century the town was noted for nail-making; Robert Plot in his book 'The Natural History of Staffordshire' (1696), states that the work of nailing kept 2,000 men and boys employed in Sedgley alone.

SEDGLEY

THE BULL RING 1968 / S336012

Standing on a limestone hill, Dudley Castle dominates the town. Rebuilt in stone in the early 12th century, Dudley was slighted in 1175 after its owner, Gervase Pagnell, chose the wrong side in a dispute between Henry II and Prince Henry. The castle passed by marriage to the de Somerys; they rebuilt the fortress in stone, including the keep, gate-house and curtain wall. During the English Civil War, Dudley was the last castle in Staffordshire to be held for the King, finally surrendering in May 1646. It was again slighted but remained habitable. In 1750 it was reduced to a ruin by fire.

DUDLEY

FROM THE CASTLE c1955 /
D103016

Here we see the castle gateway and entrance to the zoo. Opened in 1937 and set within the castle grounds, the zoo, with over 400 species, became one of the best in the country.

DUDLEY

THE CASTLE GATEWAY 1949 / D103004

This view shows Castle Street before its partial redevelopment in the 1960s. The church is St Edmund's, which was rebuilt in brick and stone in the 1720s after apparently being derelict for about eighty years. It was remodelled in the 19th century and is noted for its unusually long chancel.

DUDLEY

CASTLE STREET AND ST EDMUND'S c1955 / D103026

The developers have struck in Castle Street. Over on the left Sketchley are offering their famous same day cleaning service, and there are deals to be had at Hartley Carpets, but what's a 'chipette' when it's at home? As for The Castle, it was finished in that bleak sixties style that looked shabby before the paint was even dry, while across the road The Angel looks as solid as ever.

DUDLEY

CASTLE STREET 1968 / D103192

There is not a shop to let in sight. Mini cars appear to be
flavour of the month with the drivers of Brierley Hill. When
introduced in 1959 the Mini was radical in its design. It
was only 10 ft long, ran on 10 inch wheels, and came with
front-wheel drive and independent suspension. The battery
was in the boot.

BRIERLEY HILL

HIGH STREET c1967 / B355017

The reasoning behind the construction of the Dudley and Stourbridge Canals was for the transportation of coal from pits around Dudley to the glass works at Stourbridge, and for the export of coals and glass to other areas by means of a junction with the Staffordshire & Worcestershire Canal at Stourton. The Main Line of the Stourbridge Canal swung south and then east around Brierley Hill to meet up with the Dudley Canal at Black Delph Locks. The Dudley Canal passed through Round Oak Steel Works and continued on to join up with the Birmingham Canal via Netherton Tunnel.

BRIERLEY HILL

THE CANAL LOCKS c1965 / B355004

STOURBRIDGE

Between 1914 and 1920 there were huge increases in the price of basic foodstuffs, but by the time this picture was taken they were falling to near pre-war levels. Cheese, which had cost 8d a pound in 1914, had risen to 1s 2d by 1920. By 1931 Stourbridge housewives were paying close on 9d a pound. The price of a dozen eggs had risen from 1s 3d in 1914 to a massive 4s 6d by 1920, but had fallen back to 1s 6d.

STOURBRIDGE

HIGH STREET 1931 / 84685

Bordeaux House dominates this part of the High Street; compare it to the International Stores or the local branch of the National Provincial Bank. The two men nearest the camera on the right are standing on the pavement at Barclay's Bank corner, above which were the offices of Mellor and Ellis, the solicitors.

STOURBRIDGE

THE TOWN HALL 1931 / 84683

This view looks down Lower High Street, where the King Edward VI Grammar School can be seen on the right. In those days it was Fosters for clothes and the Corner Shop for wines, spirits, Butler's Ales, and the dreaded Armadillo sherry.

STOURBRIDGE

LOWER HIGH STREET c1960 / S213009

It is hole in the road time again as the lads from Stourbridge gas works prepare to do their stuff. In 1871 W Harrison, secretary of the Birmingham Gas Co, certainly did his stuff; he cooked the books and made off with £18,000. When the company was dissolved, £100 was left in the kitty for Harrison's prosecution in the event of his ever returning to England.

STOURBRIDGE

KIDDERMINSTER ROAD 1931 / 84689

OLD SWINFORD

THE CHURCH 1931 / 84691

Was the Millennium Dome at Greenwich based on Kingswinford shopping centre? Perhaps we should be told! This picture was taken in the days when we had real money and no one had heard of new pence. In 1967 a dozen eggs cost 4s 1d; 2lb of sugar 1s 9d; potatoes were 5d a pound; a pint of milk 10d; streaky bacon 3s 6d a pound; and for the well off, sirloin was 6s 10d a pound.

KINGSWINFORD

THE SHOPPING CENTRE c1965 / K84009

Castle Bromwich, just five miles north-east of the city, was incorporated into Birmingham in 1931. In those days it was still very much a village. To the north of the church were the remains of a motte, the village was served by the early Georgian church of St Mary and St Margaret, and nearby was Castle Bromwich Hall.

CASTLE BROMWICH

THE VILLAGE c1965 / C281006

The development of Castle Bromwich really got under way in the 1930s with the Hodgehill Common housing estate. After the second world war, in which Castle Bromwich played a major part with its Spitfire factory, there were further housing developments at Bucklands End and the Firs. About the time this picture was taken, plans by Sheppard Fidler had been accepted for a 461-acre development to include sixteen-storey tower blocks, two shopping centres, schools, community buildings and parks.

CASTLE BROMWICH

CHESTER ROAD c1965 / C281001

ASTON

The parish church of St Peter and St Paul is the only church within city limits to be mentioned in the Domesday Book. The west tower and the spire date from the 15th century, though the latter was partially rebuilt in 1776-77. The church itself was extensively remodelled in 1879-90, and further work was done in 1908 when the south aisle and porch were rebuilt.

Begun in 1618 for Sir Thomas Holte, Aston was not completed until 1635. This picture shows the east front; it comprises a main block of seven bays topped by a clock tower and two-stage cupola, and two projecting wings each with a square turret. During the English Civil War, Aston was held for the King by Sir Thomas. It is still possible to see the damage caused by Parliamentarian artillery.

ASTON

ASTON HALL 1896 / 37295

The entrance hall marks a change from those built during the Tudor period; this one is built for show rather than for use as a room. The decoration is outstanding, though the marble fireplace and animal frieze are believed to be early 19th-century. On the left can be seen two of the three archways, and between them is some of the oak panelling that rises to the height of the archway cornices.

ASTON

ASTON HALL, ENTRANCE HALL 1896 / 37298

Designed by Charles Barry, the Birmingham and Midland Institute opened in 1856, the foundation stone having been laid by Prince Albert in November 1855. The institute, which offered a range of evening classes for workers, and was famed for its penny lectures, was one of the earlier projects linked with a major redevelopment of the town centre that began in the 1850s and continued through to the 1870s.

BIRMINGHAM

PARADISE STREET 1896 / 37274

The competition to design a new town hall was won by J A Hansom and E Welsh; their outline plans were preferred to those submitted by leading architects such as Charles Barry and Thomas Rickman. Work began in 1832, but the project ran into problems owing to a serious underestimate by the builders, who eventually went bankrupt. As the architects had agreed to underwrite the builders, they too were declared bankrupt. Work continued slowly; it was not until 1850 that the building was ready for occupation.

BIRMINGHAM

THE TOWN HALL 1896 / 37275

Opened in 1885, the Art Gallery and Museum was designed by Yeoville Thomason, who had also designed the adjoining Council House. Much of the money for the gallery came from wealthy glass manufacturer Thomas Osler, whose firm made the famous glass fountain centrepiece for the Great Exhibition at the Crystal Palace. The clock tower is known as Big Brum.

BIRMINGHAM
THE ART GALLERY 1896 / 37279

BIRMINGHAM

CHRIST CHURCH 1896 / 37276

By the end of the 19th century, New Street was both the principal business street in the town and the best for shopping and entertainment. This view is from Paradise Street. On the left just off camera is Christ Church, and over to the right is the Post Office. Known as New Street since the 15th century, the oldest building extant in 1896 was probably No 29, a silversmith and jewellers, that had a rainwater head dated 1687. No 29 was demolished in 1902-03.

BIRMINGHAM

NEW STREET 1896 / 37270

This view looks towards the Town Hall. It cost one penny to travel the length of New Street by horse-drawn omnibus, while a Hansom cab cost somewhat more. Cab fares were regulated by the council: a Hansom cost one shilling for the first mile, each additional half-mile costing 4d. They could also be hired by the hour at 2s 6d for the first hour and 6d for each additional quarter hour. The Hansom was designed by J A Hansom, the architect of the Town Hall.

BIRMINGHAM

NEW STREET 1890 / B100001

New Street was the scene of many events.
Large crowds gathered along it for the laying
of the foundation stone of the Masonic
Hall. In July 1891 windows and balconies
were packed to capacity for the visit of the
Prince and Princess of Wales, who had come
to Birmingham to open the Victoria Law
Courts.

BIRMINGHAM
NEW STREET 1896 / 37271

Described in 1890 as a 'handsome modern thoroughfare',
Corporation Street was the result of a massive redevelopment
of 93 acres of slums. Councillor Ward said that the 'rubbish
and dilapidation of whole quarters have reminded me of
Strasbourg which I saw soon after the bombardment'. The area
was notorious, wells were contaminated with raw sewage, and
the death rate was 3.2 per cent above the national average.

BIRMINGHAM
CORPORATION STREET 1896 / 37269

BIRMINGHAM

CORPORATION STREET 1890 / B100002

Edgbaston is the most famous of all Birmingham's suburbs. It was the home of the Chamberlain family, who had an impact on both the development of Birmingham and the history of Britain; the headquarters of Warwickshire County Cricket Club; and the site of the Botanical Gardens. In 1949 the shops along Hagley Road were all taken. Booksellers and stationers T W Atkinson even operated a library from which books could be loaned at 2d a time.

EDGBASTON

HAGLEY ROAD 1949 / E85002

Situated 4.5 miles south of Birmingham, Bournville was chosen by George Cadbury in 1879 as the site for his new factory and for a model village for his workers. Cadbury was one of the first employers to grasp the importance of the relationship between environment and workplace. Initially 143 homes were built, which were sold at cost price. A 999 year leasing arrangement ensured that gardens and open areas could not be built on.

BOURNVILLE

MARY VALE ROAD 1949 / B354050

BOURNVILLE

THE CARILLION c1960 / B354104

King's Norton is less than two miles from Bournville, and though urban sprawl between the wars linked it to Birmingham, the old village still retains much of its rural character. The village was a part of Worcestershire until 1911, when it was absorbed into Birmingham.

KING'S NORTON

THE VILLAGE GREEN c1955 / K83008

The village church, dedicated to St Nicholas, is Norman in origin and was partially rebuilt during the 13th century. Within a few decades the church was extended; the west tower with its octagonal spire is 15th-century. The clerestory was added in the 17th century and the north aisle remodelled in the 1870s.

KING'S NORTON

THE OLD SARACEN'S HEAD 1949 / K83007

The old inn dates from the late 15th century and comprises
three bays with two wings projecting behind either side of a
courtyard. The north wing, which is jettied on a moulded
wood bressumer, remains half-timbered; the south wing was
rebuilt in the 19th century to house the parish hall.

KING'S NORTON

OLD SARACEN'S HEAD INN C1955 / K83004

The parish church of St Laurence is originally 12th-century with a
13th-century chancel. The south aisle was replaced in the late 13th
century; the north aisle was only added in 1900, though it was built
in a 14th-century style. On the right is the pound, or village lock-up,
built of sandstone.

NORTHFIELD

THE PARISH CHURCH AND GREAT STONE INN C1955 / N203003

NORTHFIELD

THE BLACK HORSE c1955 / N203007

The Great Stone Inn is one of Northfield's older drinking establishments, as is the Old Bell House, Bell Hill. Despite its looks, the Black Horse, Bristol Road, is in fact a fine mock-Tudor building designed by C E Bateman and built in 1929.

Bell Road is an echo of Northfield's agricultural past. The population grew by over 200 per cent between 1881 and 1891, nearly all of it overflow from Birmingham; but modern Northfield owes much to the opening of the Austin works at Longbridge.

NORTHFIELD

BELL ROAD c1955 / N203001

It was in February 1909 that proposals were made under the Greater Birmingham Plan to annex Aston Manor, Erdington, Handworth, King's Norton, Northfield and Yardley. The Urban District of King's Norton and Northfield had a population in excess of 78,000 and covered 22,000 acres. The plans would give Birmingham a population of 850,000, making it the second city in England.

NORTHFIELD

BRISTOL ROAD SOUTH c1955 / N203005

ACOCK'S GREEN

YARDLEY ROAD c1965 / A136014

Until the 1830s Acock's Green was a small agricultural village. Development really began in 1839 when the old estate, comprising about 150 acres, was given over to building.

Both Acock's Green and Olton were once residential areas favoured by the wealthier inhabitants of Birmingham, but they became progressively industrialized as factories opened along the route of the railway. The Birmingham Mail in November 1903 reported that Acock's Green's genteeler residents were moving further out: 'Like the Arab, they are folding their tents and stealing away in the direction of Knowle and Solihull, where the octopus tentacles of expanding Birmingham are as yet in the distance'.

ACOCK'S GREEN

YARDLEY ROAD c1965 / A136012

YARDLEY

THE UNDERPASS c1965 / Y18012

Situated to the east of Acock's Green, and four miles from the city centre, Yardley is one of the parishes absorbed by Birmingham in 1911. It is crossed by main roads to Warwick, Stratford and Coventry, and our picture harks back to those cone-free days of yester-year.

The half-timbered manor house of Blakesley Hall dates from 1575.
Yardley is an ancient manor and parish covering 11.5 square miles, and
was once a part of Worcestershire. With the extension of the tramway
from Small Heath to the Swan Hotel it became a popular residential
suburb for those businessmen wishing to live in more rural surroundings.
In 1900 the parish was still predominantly agricultural.

YARDLEY

BLAKESLEY HALL c1965 / Y18016

Of the ancient medieval parish church little remains. The red sandstone tower dates from the 15th century, and may itself have been a rebuild on the base of an earlier structure. The remainder dates from 1867 when the church was rebuilt at a cost of £3,500.

HARBORNE

ST PETER'S CHURCH c1965 / H365032

The High Street sports a branch of F W Woolworth, and the local branch of the National Provincial Bank is housed in half-timbered style premises. The church of St John Baptist was designed by Yeoville Thomason, architect of Birmingham Council House. He was also responsible for rebuilding St Peter's, Harborne.

HARBORNE

HIGH STREET c1955 / H365011

The pub on the corner was always a handy place for a quick lunchtime pint, and even in 1965 for a pie. Of Harborne's pubs, the Bell, Old Church Street has survived for three hundred years; its bar is in the passageway. The Junction, High Street has one very big room, an island bar, and some fixtures and fittings supplied by the Bass Museum.

HARBORNE

PRINCES CORNER c1965 / H365023

Whether Harborne is famous for being a good place to catch newts and minnows is not recorded, but it was famous as a place for growing gooseberries; the annual dinner of the Gooseberry Growers' Society was first held in Harborne in 1815. In the second half of the 19th century Harborne was something of a go-ahead place. In the 1880s it opened its own Institute and Masonic Hall, and one of the conditions of it joining Birmingham was that it got its own free library.

HARBORNE

GROVE PARK c1965 / H365034

REDNAL

THE STEPS, LICKY HILLS c1960 / R250071

A classic view of the three spires. The spires are those of St Michael's (295 ft), Holy Trinity (237 ft), and the octagonal steeple (230 ft) of Christ Church. Christ Church is a remnant of the Grey Friar's monastery demolished in 1539. Both Christ Church and St Michael's were bombed during the second world war.

COVENTRY

THE THREE SPIRES C1890 / C169002

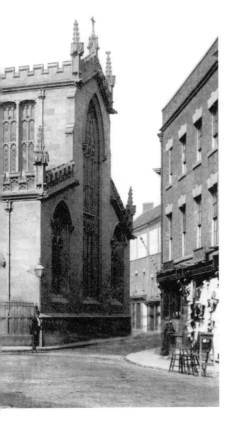

Built of red sandstone, St John's has links with Queen Isabella (1292-1358) and the Guild of St John Baptist (founded 1342). It was restored by Sir Giles Gilbert Scott in 1877, though the corbelled turrets on the tower are early 19th-century additions.

COVENTRY

ST JOHN'S CHURCH c1884 / 17127

Founded in the 12th century, the hospital of St John Baptist offered temporary relief to poor wayfarers and relief to the sick and poor of the city. St John's benefited from a number of bequests, including a weekly load of wood; this was negotiated by Roger de Montalt, Earl of Chester, when he sold off his lordship rights in the Earl's Half to the Prior. St John's was disbanded during the Reformation, and the building later used for a free school.

COVENTRY

ST JOHN'S HOSPITAL 1892 / 30919

By 1941 planning was well under way to rebuild the shattered heart of Coventry. The Broadgate shopping precinct, a series of squares with shops on two levels, was an excellent idea, even if the finished product was dull. In the picture we have two buildings from the 1930s: Lloyd's Bank (1932) with its giant arch, and the National Provincial Bank with its neo-classical portico.

COVENTRY

HIGH STREET AND BROADGATE c1955 / C169003

Sandwiched between St Nicholas Street and the old market place at Cross Cheaping, Bishop Street was one of Coventry's main shopping thoroughfares. As can be seen, the street was served by horse-drawn trams. In 1895 Coventry became one of the early converts to electric street tramways; the system operated until November 1940, when it suffered heavy damage during the blitz.

COVENTRY

BISHOP STREET 1892 / 30914

Coventry has undergone massive redevelopment since the end of the second world war, not only with projects such as the Broadgate shopping precinct, but an American-inspired partly-elevated ring-road that surrounds the old city centre. Few streets still follow their original medieval plans, though not all have been lost since 1945. Butcher Row went long ago.

COVENTRY

BUTCHER ROW 1892 / C169001

COVENTRY

BUTCHER ROW 1892 / 30916A

Two boys appear to be wearing a school uniform: boaters, jacket and starched collars. Palmer & Co, brokers and furniture dealers, have allowed their stock to flood out almost to the centre of the street in a happy confusion that would almost certainly win them the Turner Prize. Over on the left we appear to have an umbrella maker and a barber.

COVENTRY

HOLY TRINITY CHURCH 1892 / 30927

The Benedictine Priory, founded in 1043, grew to become one of the wealthiest in the midlands, and the sheer bulk of its buildings must have made an imposing sight on the Coventry skyline. The complex included a church about 400 ft long; a cloister on the north side; the west front was supported by towers or turrets; and there were two chapels radiating off from the chancel.

COVENTRY

THE BLUE COAT SCHOOL AND PRIORY RUINS c1890 / c169301

Holy Trinity, with its superb timbered ceilings, 15th-century stone pulpit, brass eagle lectern, and octagonal font with panelled stem, is one of just a handful of buildings that survive from Coventry's medieval past. The interior underwent restoration in the 1850s.

COVENTRY

HOLY TRINITY CHURCH 1892 / 30928

COVENTRY

ST MICHAEL'S CHURCH c1884 / 17124

This was the parish church in the Earl's Half; with a floor area of 24,000 sq ft, St Michael's was one of the most impressive and possibly the largest parish church in England. St Michael's housed six chapels belonging to the town's dyers, cappers, mercers, smiths, girdlers, and drapers.

When Basil Spence designed the new cathedral, he incorporated the ruins of St Michael's into the scheme of things: the old church in effect became the new cathedral's vestibule. Spence's design was attacked by traditionalists for being too modern; others saw it as a statement of Coventry's renewal following the blitz. His use of curves helped to disguise the fact that the nave of the new building was only 270 ft long and 80 ft wide: quite small in cathedral terms. By the entrance is Epstein's St Michael and Lucifer, one of his last works.

COVENTRY

THE CATHEDRAL c1965 / C169076

COVENTRY

ST MARY'S HALL 1892 / 30929

COVENTRY

ST MARY'S HALL 1892 / 30930

The stocks, along with the pillory and the whipping post, were instruments of punishment at one time in use throughout England. The stocks were usually positioned on a main thoroughfare, or better still in the market place; convicted wrongdoers were secured in them by either their legs or arms. Punishment might well involve several sessions in the stocks on consecutive market days.

COVENTRY

THE STOCKS, ST MARY'S HALL c1890 / c169302

In 1509 William Ford, a merchant, founded and endowed the Greyfriar's Hospital, a half-timbered almshouse for five poor men and their wives. It was just one of a number of generous donations made to the city during the 16th century; others included Bond's (Bablake) Hospital for poor men founded in 1506, and Bablake Boys' Hospital in 1560.

COVENTRY

FORD'S HOSPITAL 1892 / 30918

COVENTRY

FORD'S HOSPITAL 1892 / 30917

Once a canal feeder, Chasewater was developed for recreational purposes in the late 1950s offering sailing and boating. In 1967 it was the venue for the world's first 24-hour international powerboat race. Since 1966 Chasewater has been the home of the Chasewater Light Railway Co, whose line runs alongside the reservoir.

CHASEWATER

c1965 / C280006

Invented by Christopher Cockerell, the Hovercraft is propelled on a cushion of air and can travel with ease over land, swamp, marshy ground or water. When this picture was taken there were very few privately-built Hovercraft around, so this one was bound to draw attention to itself.

CHASEWATER

HOVERCRAFT c1965 / C280005

The ornate fountain and clock tower forms the centrepiece of the Market Place, but it looks as though Willenhall will soon have another attraction, the Zorba Grill—no doubt inspired by the film starring Anthony Quinn.

WILLENHALL

MARKET PLACE c1965 / W238010

SUTTON COLDFIELD

SUTTON PARK c1960 / S339039

Sutton Park was one of the largest in Warwickshire, over 2,000 acres of woodlands and lakes. The park made the town something of a tourist attraction. During Whit-week 1882 the town had over 19,000 visitors; in 1883 it had 11,300; and in 1884 it had 17,400.

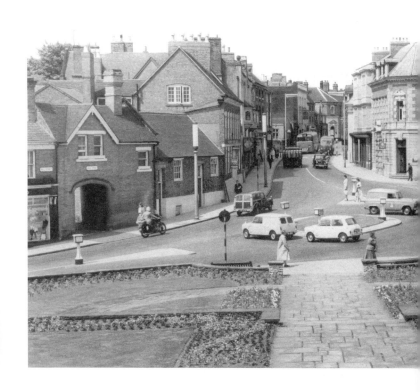

SUTTON COLDFIELD

HIGH STREET c1965 / S339055

An old market town on the road to Lichfield, only seven miles from
Birmingham, Sutton Coldfield hung on to its independence until annexed by
its large neighbour in 1974. Though an important town in the Middle Ages,
Sutton Coldfield's development took off in the 16th century thanks to John
Veysey. A local man, John was eventually appointed Bishop of Exeter.

SUTTON COLDFIELD

THE PARADE 1949 / S339006

SUTTON COLDFIELD

THE PARADE c1949 / S339003

In 1885 Solihull was described as a 'very pleasant village, but a few miles distant'. Even so, the population then was about 6000. The town's development received a boost in 1945 when Rover announced their intention to abandon their Coventry plant and concentrate production at their former shadow factory at Solihull.

SOLIHULL

HIGH STREET 1968 / S257084

As with many other towns, the centre of Solihull was redeveloped in the 1960s. Among the projects was a new civic centre designed by H Weedon & Partners, and the demolition of Drury Lane for a pedestrian shopping precinct.

SOLIHULL

MELL SQUARE c1965 / S257022

Shirley became a location for a number of industries, and two buildings in particular stand out. The first, in Cranmore Boulevard, is an office range built in 1954-56 for Carrs and designed by Erno Goldfinger. The second, designed by Clifford Tee & Gale and built in 1963-65, is the research labs of Joseph Lucas Ltd on Stratford Road opposite Cranmore Boulevard.

SHIRLEY

STRATFORD ROAD c1955 / S337001

Knowle, one mile south-east of Solihull, contains several interesting old buildings, including the medieval Chester House, and the heavily restored 17th-century Red Lion. This scene looks very quiet, but it wasn't always so. One Sunday in 1945 a tremendous explosion rocked the village, and a ball of flames erupted from behind the trees on Warwick Road. A Mosquito aircraft had crashed after developing engine trouble.

KNOWLE

WARWICK ROAD c1965 / K120017

KNOWLE

TOP LOCK c1965 / K120007

At Knowle a flight of locks raises the canal nearly 42 ft. A flight of five wide locks were built in the 1930s to replace six narrow ones; they can be seen here side-by-side. There are also a number of side ponds here, which date back to the original canal and were built to conserve water.

INDEX

PLEASE HELP US BRING FRITH'S PHOTOGRAPHS TO LIFE

Our authors do their best to recount the history of the places they write about. They give insights into how particular towns and villages developed, they describe the architecture of streets and buildings, and they discuss the lives of famous people who lived there. But however knowledgeable our authors are, the story they tell is necessarily incomplete.

Frith's photographs are so much more than plain historical documents. They are living proofs of the flow of human life down the generations. They show real people at real moments in history; and each of those people is the son or daughter of someone, the brother or sister, aunt or uncle, grandfather or grandmother of someone else. All of them lived, worked and played in the streets depicted in Frith's photographs.

We would be grateful if you would tell us about the many places shown in our photographs—the streets with their buildings, shops, businesses and industries. Describe your own memories of life in those streets: what it was like growing up there, who ran the local shop and what shopping was like years ago; if your workplace is shown tell us about your working day and what the building is used for now. With your help more and more Frith photographs can be brought to life, and vital memories preserved for posterity.

We will gradually add your comments and stories to the archive for the benefit of historians of the future. Wherever possible, we will try to include some of your comments in future editions of our books. Moreover, if you spot errors in dates, titles or other facts, please let us know, because our archive records are not always completely accurate—they rely on 150 years of human endeavour and hand-compiled records.

So please write, fax or email us with your stories and memories. Thank you!

CHOOSE ANY PHOTOGRAPH FROM THIS BOOK

for your FREE Mounted Print. Order further prints at half price

Fill in and cut out the voucher on the next page and return it with your remittance for £2.50 for postage, packing and handling to UK addresses (US $5.00 for USA and Canada). For all other overseas addresses include £5.00 post and handling. Choose any photograph included in this book. Make sure you quote its unique reference number eg. 42365 (it is mentioned after the photograph date. 1890 / 42365). Your SEPIA print will be approx 12" x 8" and mounted in a cream mount with a burgundy rule line (overall size 14" x 11").

Mounted Print
Overall size 14 x 11 inches

Order additional Mounted Prints at HALF PRICE - If you would like to order more Frith prints from this book, possibly as gifts for friends and family, you can buy them at half price (with no extra postage and handling costs) - only £7.49 each (UK orders), US $14.99 each (USA and Canada).

* IMPORTANT!

These special prices are only available if you order at the same time as you order your free mounted print. You must use the ORIGINAL VOUCHER on the facing page (no copies permitted). We can only despatch to one address.

Have your Mounted Prints framed (UK orders only) - For an extra £14.95 per print you can have your mounted print(s) framed in an elegant polished wood and gilt moulding, overall size 16" x 13" (no additional postage).

FRITH PRODUCTS AND SERVICES

All Frith photographs are available for you to buy as framed or mounted prints. From time to time, other illustrated items such as Address Books, Calendars, Table Mats are also available. Already, almost 50,000 Frith archive photographs can be viewed and purchased on the internet through the Frith website.

For more detailed information on Frith companies and products, visit

www.francisfrith.co.uk

For further information, trade, or author enquiries, contact:

The Francis Frith Collection, Frith's Barn, Teffont, Salisbury SP3 5QP
Tel: +44 (0) 1722 716 376 Fax: +44 (0) 1722 716 881 Email: sales@francisfrith.co.uk

Voucher

for FREE and Reduced Price Frith Prints

Do not photocopy this voucher. Only the original is valid, so please fill it in, cut it out and return it to us with your order.

Picture ref no	Page number	Qty	Mounted @ £7.49 UK @$14.99 US	Framed + £14.95 (UK only)	US orders Total $	UK orders Total £
1		1	Free of charge*	£	$	£
2			£7.49 ($14.99)	£	$	£
3			£7.49 ($14.99)	£	$	£
4			£7.49 ($14.99)	£	$	£
5			£7.49 ($14.99)	£	$	£
6			£7.49 ($14.99)	£	$	£
Please allow 28 days for delivery			* Post & handling		$5.00	£2.50
			Total Order Cost US $			£

Title of this book . . . .

I enclose a cheque / postal order (UK) for £ . . . . $ . . . .
payable to 'Francis Frith Collection' (USA orders 'Frith USA Inc')

OR debit my Mastercard / Visa / Switch (UK) / Amex card / Discover (USA)
(credit cards only on non UK and US orders), card details below

Card Number

Issue No (Switch only)   Valid from (Amex/Switch)

Expires   Signature

Name Mr/Mrs/Ms . . . .

Address . . . .

. . . .

. . . .

Postcode/Zip. . . . . Country . . . .

Daytime Tel No . . . .   Valid to 31/12/06

PAYMENT CURRENCY: We only accept payment in £ Sterling or US $. If you are ordering **from any other country, please pay by credit card**, and you will be charged in one of these currencies.